CW01582235

Whispers of Womb and Wilderness

A collection of art and poems by Nicole B Roberts

Copyright © 2024 by Nicole B Roberts
Library of Congress Control Number: 2024903041

ISBN:
978-1-7350804-7-5 (Hardback)
978-1-7350804-8-2 (Paperback)
978-1-7350804-9-9 (Ebook)

All rights reserved.
No part of this book may be reproduced or transmitted in any form or by any means, electronic or mechanical, including photocopying, recording, or by an information storage and retrieval system, without permission in writing from the copyright owner.

For inquiries, address:
nicole.the.creative.catalyst@gmail.com.

First edition published in the United States of America
April 2024
by
The Creative Catalyst LLC
www.TheCreativeCatalyst.Art

For our daughters

May you dare to follow your whispers.
May you have strength for the journey of the womb and the wilderness.
May you remember the wisdom buried within.

NBR

Whispers

Womb

Wilderness

Wisdom

Introduction

In September of 2021 my little sister sent me a t-shirt and this note in the mail.

Dear Nicole,

I saw these shirts & HAD to get us some. We have an ancestor that was accused of witchcraft in Massachusetts in the 1600's. She was born in England in 1594. Winnifred Lovering Henchman Holman. She started helping people w/ herbs etc to support her family – her husband had died. One neighbor's daughters died despite her best efforts. So they claimed she was a witch. She was put in jail. BUT– somehow she was able to get signatures from many prominate men in the community saying she was a good woman + not a witch. She used this in her trial, was found NOT guilty & the neighbor lady got tried for slander.

Winnifred went free + resumed her medicine + midwifery. She was a "witch" they could not burn.

I love you + your strength, character + grit. I am proud to be your sister!

♡ Amy

P.S. They sent an XL ☹ not L! So sorry. Hoping it will shrink.

We are the granddaughters of the witches they could not burn.
Our mothers and grandmothers overcame so many challenges so we could be here in a time when we are no longer burned at the stake for speaking our truth.
And yet, so often we are still afraid to do so. I knew then, I needed to do something to honor the feminine nature that had been controlled, contorted and silenced for so long.
But who was I to do anything so bold?

I remembered the phrase, "Start where you are, use what you have, do what you can." Because art is how I process life, creating a new collection felt like the first right thing. So, over the next month I drew a new piece of art every day, each exploring the shadowy edges, the whispers, of the feminine. Many pieces became recurrent self-portraits as I tried to step into these characters and feelings completely.

Once I was finished with this body of work, I knew sitting with each piece of art and listening for what it was trying to say felt like the next right thing. I made a vow to myself that I would let the words be whatever they wanted to be.

As the first few writings emerged, it became clear the whispers wanted to be poems and there was a hidden structure to it all. I pinned everything to my wall and saw there were four main ideas that corresponded with the four feminine archetypes that were woven and overlapped throughout them all:

whispers (the maiden),
womb (the mother),
wilderness (the wild woman),
wisdom (the wise woman).

It felt surreal to see a pattern to what felt like madness. It felt like a sliver of redemption for all the women before me. I felt honored to be the one holding the pen and to have my face representing their stories. I was overwhelmed with gratitude that I had chosen to take this path without knowing where it would lead.

My desire is that this collection of art and words will show you, precious reader, that you are not alone. I pray it will remind you of your worthiness and inspire you to step into your power. Above all, my hope is that you will hear my voice and choose to use your own.

With love and adoration,
Nicole B Roberts

Whispers

The Map

Look around child,
There are secrets in the seasons.
Look up child,
The moon makes a map.
Look within child,
The womb holds wisdom withheld from the world.
Know child,
You are the keeper and the key.

Messenger

A Vessel, A Warrior, A Messenger for Man
Mimicking the moon, the seasons, the plan
The Maker's secret army
Has been quietly formed
A bigger purpose has been waiting
Since the day that we were born
Sophia, Eve, Mary and me
From alpha to omega-
The invisible She
Masked, buried, identity unspoken
One bite of the apple
And they thought that we were broken
But, the seed of truth
Made camp in our wombs
The pattern of creation
Forever entombed
We became the vessels
With a message deep inside
Warriors the world needed
But strategically denied
Ezer Kenegdo
Go back to the start
Remember the identity
God planted in our heart
Wisdom will find us wherever we go
Our purpose is waiting
Be still and know

One Answer

Curiosity is the purest religion
The path of a million questions
That reunites us with the whole
Where we discover that there is
Only one answer
To everything

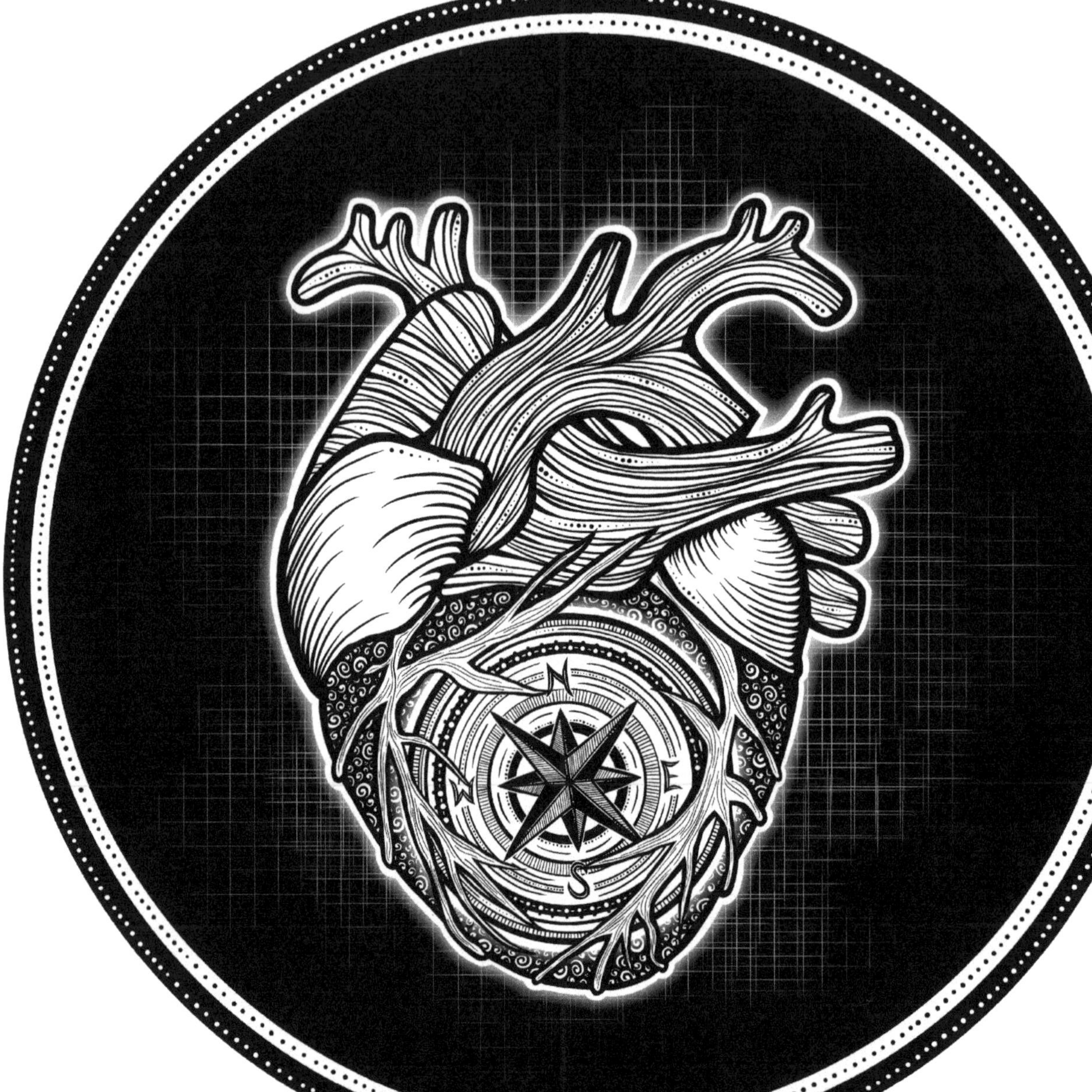

Compass

The universe hides a compass deep within us
And waits for us to find it.

For much of our meandering,
We do not notice how it pulls us along.

But in moments of lightning strike emotion,
When our chest tightens and swells,
When our eyes burn with wet knowing,
When our breath catches
Threatening to burst us apart with its tingling tension,
When our insides thunder
With deafening desire and anxious hope
When we forget our fears for a frozen instant,
Immune to conditions and timelines.

These undiluted magnetic pulls
Are the hallowed echoes of our own compass heart
Guiding us toward the path of our purpose.

Gallery

Nature is God in all things
Hear the buzz of the honeybee wings
Everything a gallery of divine power
Seasons, faces, the budding of a flower

The golden ratio
The God equation
Masculine and feminine
In synchronized creation
The structure of the universe is
Everywhere we look
Truth isn't exclusive
To buildings and books

Look around at the world
With the eyes of a child
See the structure in the madness
The intention in the wild
"By their fruits ye shall know them"
Connect each clue
You'll find the truth
That God is in you

Thirst

You are the wellspring of the world
The cyclic flowing source
Of passion, pleasure and procreation–
The living waters of love

There is an unquenchable thirst
For your animating presence
For you hold the power of life
In your hands, heart and womb
A gift infinitely yours to give–
Goddess of creation

Sui Generis

Elevation

Isolation
can create
Elevation
if we allow our
Separation
to gift us with
Inspiration
rather than
Desperation
for others
Validation.

We discover our
Emancipation
when we gift others with
Exoneration,
no longer requiring their
Participation
or outward
Motivation
to ascend to our next
Iteration
and embrace our unique
Destination.

Blueprint

Soaking up the structure.
Absorbing the order.
Basking in the blueprint.
Holding space for holiness.
Doing nothing and everything
In the same moment.
Knowing wholeness.

Blind

She is not invisible,
The world has made us blind.

Serpents, roses, bees and trees–
Her whispers intertwined.
They slither and bloom,
They buzz and unfurl,
Patiently waiting for our eyes to be freed.

You can keep your blinding books
With words of dusty men,

I'm busy watching bees on buds,
Collecting snake sheds from the weeds.
I'm busy climbing branch and limb
To meet Her on the breeze.

For once you've glanced the truth of Her
You can't go blind again.
Once you've glimpsed her infinite womb,
The world's lies can never win.

Womb

Infinity

I am the succulent, teasing sprout of spring.
I am the savory, smiling sweat of summer.
I am the whispering, whipping wind of fall.
I am the deep, desperate stop of winter.

I am the seasons
Wrapped in the moon-bathed cloak of a woman.
I am a mirror of lunar perfection,
tucked in the treasure box of femininity.

I am creation, created, creating, creator.
I create.
Always.
Endlessly.
Without trying.
Without explanation.
Without want, need, or permission.

I am the womb of a woman.
I am the story of infinity.

Alchemy

I am chaos
You are control
Two bodies
One soul

Alone we languish power
No balance
No golden ratio
No duality

Together
We become creation
Conceiving consciousness
In infinite spiraling alchemy

Womb and Wilderness

There is a womb in the wilderness.
There is a wilderness in the womb.
The stories of women are stored here,
Seeds that wait for fertile ears.

Waiting for the whispering hour
When they can be spoken out loud,
Can be written down,
Can be redeemed through remembering,
Can at last make tangling roots.

    They are getting louder.
Can you hear them? These stories that stir in our bones?
    They are getting louder.
Can you feel them? The thousand-year-old tales that feel like our own?
    They are getting louder.
Do you dare to live out loud and set your self and sisters free?
    They are getting louder.
Are you bold enough to risk it all to go from I to we?

    We are getting louder.
We are the voice of the womb and the wilderness,
The swelling cyclic song of destruction and creation,
A ballad of blood and brokenness,
Bound and braided with rapturous renewal,
Every soliloquy significant and sanctified in our shared Psalm,
One story that belongs to us all.

Within

Within my womb
Exists the entire universe
The pulsating perfection of a soul
Cocooning in matter and purpose
Infinite energy metamorphosing
Becoming its most potent manifestation
With each unveiled palpitation
Of your quickening flutter heart

Invisible

I carry the weight of the world on my shoulders.
Exhaustion crushing to the bone,
Pushing me to the raw edge of everything I think I am.

In my weakest moments I cry out to her,
The invisible mother that knows.
I weep and wail and beg for an easier way,
She anchors me through anguish,
She steadies me through suffering,
She teaches me tenacity through tears,
She rocks me, whispering truths of identity forgotten,
She renews me day by day.

I persevere.
Purpose eclipsing pain,
Love bolstering the load I bear,
Gratitude reborn,
Identity remembered.

Emancipation

Wisdom is knowing
When you have reached the threshold
Of holding on and letting go.

Then choosing to let go.

To cling instead
To the faith
That the created
Will become the creator.

Trusting that the endowment of illuminating love
Is the kind that can't go out.
And that eternity hinges
On intentional emancipation.

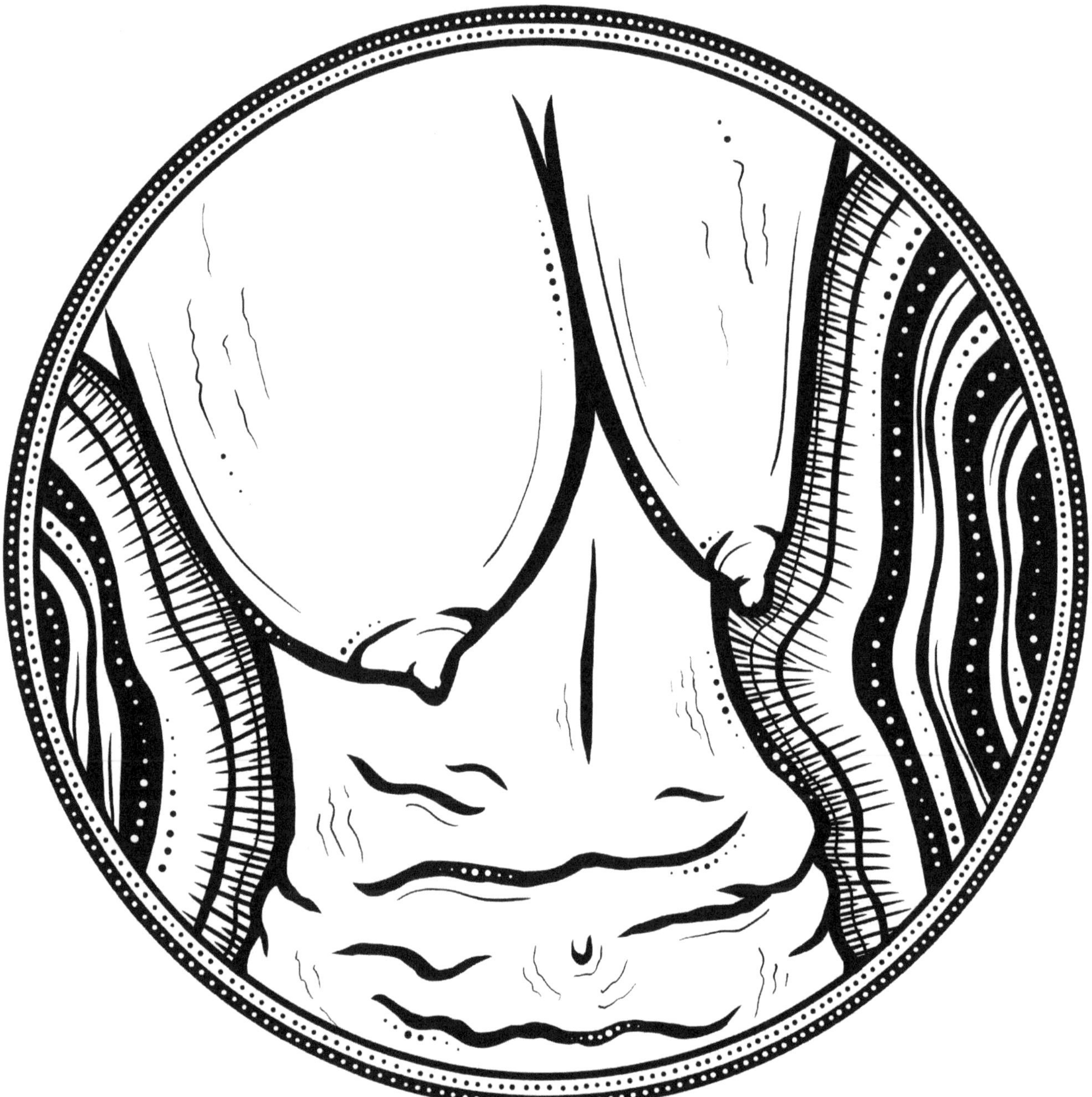

Monument

Beautiful belly,
Sagging and swaying
Where my womb
Once stretched with the miraculous,
Where babies bloomed,
Where heaven touched earth
And creator and creation were one
Where the perfect rhythm of life
Beat and bellowed like a hand-stretched drum.

Beautiful belly,
You were the vessel worthy of containing all this.
... And I am sorry.
I am sorry for seeing you as less than you are.
I am sorry for resenting you for changing,
When change is exactly what I asked of you
Beautiful belly,
I will no longer condemn you,
I will let your lines tell stories
Like the holy book that you are,
And I will honor you as a monument of initiation
Into the divine call
Of Mother.

Survive

Because I love you deeply
And want for you to thrive
I won't shield you from the darkness
I will teach you to survive

My job is not to keep you
A time will come that you must go
I'll offer everything I have
So you can learn and grow

I expect that it will pain me
When you disappear from sight
But I'll gather peace in knowing
My life gifted yours with flight

Wilderness

Frontier

I am not afraid of the dark anymore
Because I know that the light is inside me
I am a burning torch
Universal truth flanks me
Like moths to a flame

The wilderness beckons me inward
Inviting me on a journey through this darkness
After so much searching
I know it's the last frontier of truth
The one most people are afraid to step into
The one that connects all the dots
The final puzzle piece that makes us whole and free
If we are brave enough to
Embrace the loneliness so deeply
That it becomes our wisest friend

Bones

Deep In our bones it stirs
An ancient warrior spirit
Hungry
Cozy conformity has kept us comatose
The battle call is rising
Blood turning hot
The first war we must win is inside us
Break the shackles and emerge
Child of shield maidens
Remember who you are
Trade in your sword for the weapon of words
Wield them with reverent wisdom
Drop your shield, but do not cower
Own your braids and your feminine power
Our task is not to conquer distant lands
But broken minds and bloody hands
We sail the vastness of what the world thinks
Our faith in a truth that cannot sink
Danger circles and pushes us back
Trying to silence our growing attack
We see a world that others cannot
And so we forge on with a passion white-hot
We smell change just beyond fear
Hopes of our children linger near
Our path's a far cry from tidy and neat
But in victory we will know
That danger is sweet

Starry-Eyed

The darkness is not our enemy,
The blindness is.
The darkness cannot defeat us
Unless we lose sight of the light.
We CAN navigate the blackest night,
Not by trusting the stars in the skies,
but the stars in our eyes.

We were created with light inside us.
We are lanterns with hot white heat.
We are the ones who must combat the blindness.
We are the starry-eyed.
Alone or together, we will navigate this night.
Alone or together, we must be the light.

One thing is certain, one thing we know,
When light shows up, the darkness will go.
Until that time comes, we choose to stand,
With stars in our eyes and hope in our hands.

You can be
anything you choose,
as long as you
STAY INSIDE
THE BOX.
Sincerely,
Your Government,
Your Culture,
Your Religion

Blow Torch

Conformity is a cage.
Conviction is just fear in its Sunday best.
Curiosity is faith with work boots on.
We are not here to bolster a broken system,
We are here to burn it down.
Our voice is our blow torch.

Holy War

I stare into the eyes of my shadow self.
The voices outside me say I will never be whole until I destroy her.
They say I should
Hate her
Hide her
Shame her
Condemn her
And fight her.
She stares back.
Her eyes echo the same story.
As if she too was told she must destroy me in order to be whole.

And in this holy instant
We both dare to pause and wonder why we are enemies.
We sit in the sacred silence,
Staring into the inverted mirror of our soul,
Studying,
Seeking,
Knowing and fully known.

The scorching flame of fear slowly turns to ash and smoke
And we find we must embrace each other
If we are to survive the bitter chill of an illusory world.
Compelled by the catalyst of blossoming unconditional love,
We marry the darkness and the light inside us
And free ourself from the holy war within.

Messengers

Born into a man-made world, I am forced to play a game my body does not know.
I become a contortionist, an expert at bending to belong.
To survive, I shrink my knowing. I build iron clad walls around my heart.
Desperate to stop the pain of being ripped in opposite directions,
I over-indulge and over-commit to drown out the whispers.
I am praised for conforming at all costs, for mastering the motions of a game I wasn't built to win.

But beneath my fabricated fortress, the dissonance amplifies.
The conflict surges and swells like bubbling lava, cracking my sky-high barricade,
Letting poison seep into every cell.

I unfurl, I explode. Fits of rage and madness.Volcanic emotions spew.
Hot ash scorching everything I touch. In a frenzy, I release my knowing.
I rip the gag from her mouth and she gasps, this is not the poison; this is the cleansing.

I inhale her words deep into my bones. I let them sit like sponges, soaking up the mess inside me.
And I remember.
These are not moments of weakness, but moments of warning.
They are not here to destroy me, they are here to destroy the walls I built that kept them out.
I can finally hear the whispers.
Giving me permission to stop playing the game I will never win.
Beckoning me towards the world that has always been within.
Undulating to the wise song of the womb.
Untwisting to the untamed dance of the wilderness.
Unveiling the map that returns me to myself.

Quill

I hold the quill
I write my story
I can choose shame
Or I can choose glory

I can stay anchored
On shores that are safe
Or sail seas of monsters
And shape my own fate

There will be battles
But I choose the ending
Victors are made
By their own penning

Each page a new chance
To decide who I'll be
Each word builds the book
The book that is me

Unbecoming

Trapped by illusion,
They taught me to fear the flames.
They told me I would be destroyed by them.

But the heat and light beckoned
Until finally,
I stood in the spire of licking tendrils
too curious to leave.

I felt attachments to form and identity
Spark, ignite, then burn away.
Impurities implanted in my system
From a fear-fueled world
Purged by this pyre of purification.

And then...
A blistering unbecoming
An inferno of integration
A searing initiation
A scintillating emergence
  of united flesh and flame
A luminous ascension

This rapture, this resurrection, this rebirth
Was infinitely mine to claim.
Forever perched on the other side of fear.

Wisdom

Seeker

I am a wanderer towards wisdom
Seeking Sophia
The wilderness strips me of the world's weights
I find my wounds imagined
The loneliness washes my clouded eyes
I find her fingerprints abound
The masses call me lost
The mother calls me found

VERITAS
NUNQUAM
PERIT

Woven

A double helix
Of tragedy and triumph
Woven into DNA
Building blocks
That create our character

Like paper and ink
Two tools together
That become the story of our lives
Existing fully
Only with each other

Meet Her

If you wish to know God
Take your nose from your book
She'll meet you in nature
If you simply look

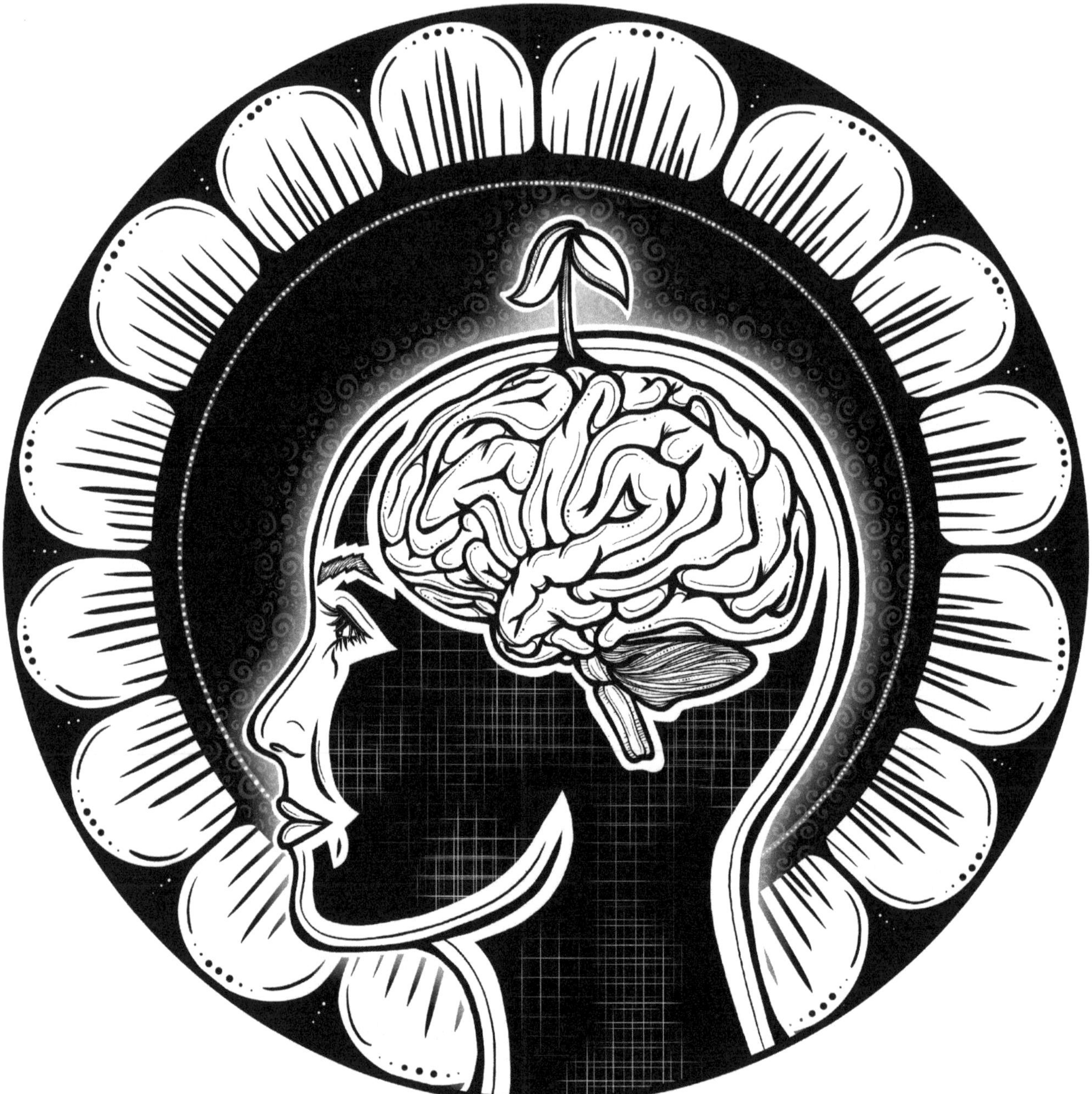

Sprout

To Sprout
    Kill your doubt
To Grow
    Find your flow
To Flower
    Know your power
To Sow
    Let it go

Lasso

We must dare to lasso the infinite
To contain the endless expanse of possibility into something tangible
A sliver small enough to fit within the human experience
Something easily digestible to the hungry soul

And then...

We must dare to question the tangible
To see the cut marks and intuitively know
It is but a sliver of infinite consciousness
An invitation to seek the source
To be born again into a less confined
Liberated realm of understanding

This is the dance of creativity
Expansion into enlightenment
Containment into form
A ladder up, a ladder down
The double helix of divine DNA
An infinite reflection of creator and created
Endlessly finding joy
In the rediscovery of each other

Expansion

Some face the sunshine
Some face the rain
Some learn from joy
Some learn from pain

We grow through what we go through
It just doesn't look the same
The only goal is expansion
That is why we came

Time

I was here before you
And after I'll remain
This moment in the middle
Is just a cosmic game

But I will use you wisely
for as long as I am here
I will love so full and fiercely
That death will hold no fear

Wounds

Hurt	to	Hope
Pain	to	Power
Mess	to	Message
Wounds	to	Wisdom

Alpha

I looked for her outside myself
Through many different seasons.
I thought I'd find her in another
For many different reasons.

As I read, and prayed and wandered,
Asking where to go,
Each day I grew more weary
Because no one seemed to know.

Did this person exist at all,
One deserving of my allegiance?
My intuition surged with knowing
And nurtured me through
My fear-fueled grievance.

I leaned on faith and somehow knew
That time would aide my quest,
I immersed myself in each new day
And in the present, I found rest.

I weathered life's storms,
Took paths of all kinds,
I sleighed giants of man
And demons of mind.

Near journey's end, I came to a mirror,
I knew the truth I sought was here.
I searched the wisdom in my own eyes,
I saw the answer buried inside.

I was the one I'd been seeking
Made worthy by my intention
I held the power all along,
Despite the world's conventions.

I journeyed the depths to find myself,
The paradox left me grinning,
I was the alpha made to lead,
I was my own beginning.

About the author

Nicole B Roberts is an award-winning artist, an author/illustrator and a free-spirited creator. She lives in Midland, Tx with her husband Tim, their three children and more pets than she ever saw coming.

Raised beneath the mountains in West Jordan, UT by an outdoorsman/ book salesman and an artist/ elementary school teacher likely sparked her lifelong love of learning.

She is ever inspired by nature, color, cycles, symbolism, growth, finding the good in people, authenticity, vulnerability, the magic of words and above all, love.

Her purpose in all she does is to model and reiterate that we were each "created to create" and that our joy is hiding within the acceptance of that divine identity.

You can see which creative squirrels she is chasing next at:
TheCreativeCatalyst.Art

Connect

nicole.the.creative.catalyst@gmail.com

TheCreativeCatalyst.Art

The.Creative.Catalyst

TheCreativeCatalyst

TheCreativeCaty

The Creative Catalyst

Titles

Figaro The Sock Fox, 2016
Creative Magic (Ebook Only), 2020
Catalyst Ranch, 2020
Catalyst Gardens, 2020
Dreamer, 2020
Whispers of Womb and Wilderness, 2024

Special Thanks

Amy Jorgensen   Melissa Heath   Sonia Castillo

Each of these women are so precious to me.
They met me in my vulnerability and showed up with empathy, encouragement and love.
They offered me the gift of a lifetime by seeing me.

Girls Who Write

This group reignited my purpose and pushed me to practice what I preach.
Having a community of like-minded women in my corner
has made me stronger, braver and more resilient.

Tim

I never would have felt safe to explore my feminine nature
without your provision and protection.
The world sees the fruits, but you were the one watering the roots.

Roman, Regan and Renly

You are forever my greatest creations and my inspiration
to push myself outside of my comfort zone so I can show you the way.

May you dare to follow your whispers

Milton Keynes UK
Ingram Content Group UK Ltd.
UKHW050100290324
440326UK00004B/104

9 781735 080475